DATE DUE

Kurt Warner

by A. R. Schaefer

Reading Consultant:
Dr. Robert Miller
Professor of Special Education
Minnesota State University, Mankato

CAPSTONE
HIGH-INTEREST
BOOKS

an imprint of Capstone Press
Mankato, Minnesota

Y
B
WAR

Capstone High-Interest Books are published by Capstone Press
151 Good Counsel Drive, P.O. Box 669, Mankato, Minnesota 56002
http://www.capstone-press.com

Library of Congress Cataloging-in-Publication Data
Schaefer, A. R. (Adam Richard), 1976–
    Kurt Warner/by A.R. Schaefer.
    p. cm.—(Sports heroes)
    Summary: A brief biography of the All-Pro quarterback for the St. Louis Rams,
Kurt Warner.
    Includes bibliographical references and index.
    ISBN 0-7368-1295-4 (hardcover)
    1. Warner, Kurt, 1971—Juvenile literature. 2. Football players—United States—
Biography—Juvenile literature. [1. Warner, Kurt, 1971– 2. Football players.] I. Title.
II. Sports heroes (Mankato, Minn.)
GV939.W36 S35 2003
796.332'092—dc21   2001008184

Editorial Credits
Matt Doeden, editor; Karen Risch, product planning editor; Timothy Halldin, series
    designer; Gene Bentdahl, book designer; Jo Miller, photo researcher

Photo Credits
Al Bello/Getty Images, 4, 35
Andy Lyons/Getty Images, 7, 41
Brian Bahr/Getty Images, 36
Charlier Neigerall/AP/Wide World Photos, 24
Craig Jones/Getty Images, 23
Donald Miralle/Getty Images, 32
Eliot Schechter/Getty Images, 38
Elsa/Getty Images, 21, 42
Jonathan Daniel/Getty Images, 28
Michael Zito/SportsChrome-USA, 18
Rob Tringali Jr./SportsChrome-USA, 9, 27, 31
Scott Halleran/Getty Images, cover
SportsChrome-USA, 10, 12
University of Northern Iowa, 14, 16

1 2 3 4 5 6 07 06 05 04 03 02

Table of Contents

CHAPTER 1

Super Bowl Hero

On January 30, 2000, the St. Louis Rams were playing the Tennessee Titans in the Super Bowl in Atlanta, Georgia. The Rams' starting quarterback was Kurt Warner. Kurt had been a starter in the NFL for only one season. In that season, he had gone from an unknown player to one of the league's biggest stars.

The Rams led 9-0 at halftime. In the third quarter, Kurt threw a 9-yard touchdown pass to wide receiver Torry Holt. The extra point gave the Rams a 16-0 lead. But the Titans did

Kurt Warner led the Rams to the Super Bowl in his first year as a starter.

not give up. They scored two touchdowns and a field goal to tie the game.

Less than two minutes remained in the game. The Rams were at their own 27-yard line. Kurt took the snap and dropped back. He saw wide receiver Isaac Bruce downfield. Kurt made a perfect pass. Bruce caught the ball in full stride. He ran into the end zone to give the Rams a 23-16 lead.

The Titans had one last chance. They drove down the field. With six seconds left, receiver Kevin Dyson caught a pass at the 5-yard line. He ran toward the end zone. Ram defensive back Mike Jones hit Dyson. Dyson stretched his arm out. But he was one yard short. The final seconds ticked away. The Rams' players and coaches ran onto the field. They were the Super Bowl champions.

Kurt was named the Super Bowl's Most Valuable Player (MVP). His total of 414 passing yards was a Super Bowl record.

Kurt held the Lombardi Trophy after the Rams defeated the Titans to win the Super Bowl.

About Kurt Warner

Kurt is an All-Pro quarterback for the St. Louis Rams. He is one of the most successful and popular players in the NFL. He was named the NFL's MVP after the 1999 and 2001 seasons.

Kurt also is successful off the field. In 2000, he signed a four-year contract extension with the Rams. The contract is worth more than $46 million. He earns millions of dollars more for endorsing products such as Campbell's Soup. Kurt also wrote an autobiography about his life called *All Things Possible*. He even has a video game named after him.

CAREER STATISTICS

Kurt Warner

NFL Passing Statistics

Year	Team	Games	Comp%	Yards	TDs	Int	Rating
1998	STL	1	36.4	39	0	0	47.2
1999	STL	16	65.1	4,353	41	13	109.2
2000	STL	11	67.7	3,429	21	18	98.3
2001	STL	16	68.7	4,830	36	22	101.4
Career		44	66.9	12,651	98	53	103.0

CHAPTER 2

The Early Years

Kurtis Eugene Warner was born June 22, 1971, in Burlington, Iowa. He is the second son of Gene and Sue Warner. Kurt lived in Cedar Rapids, Iowa, with his parents and older brother, Matt.

When Kurt was 4, his parents divorced. Kurt and Matt lived with their mother most of the time. They also spent time with Gene and his new wife, Mimi. Mimi had a son named Matt Post. Kurt and his brother often spent time with Matt.

Kurt was born June 22, 1971.

A HERO'S HERO

Joe Montana

As he grew up, Kurt admired athletes from many sports. Quarterback Joe Montana was one of his favorites. Kurt dreamed of playing quarterback like Montana.

Montana played college football at the University of Notre Dame in Indiana. In 1977, he led Notre Dame to the NCAA football championship. The San Francisco 49ers drafted Montana in 1979. He led the 49ers to four Super Bowl titles. He was named the Super Bowl MVP three times. He also won the NFL MVP award twice.

Montana ended his career with the Kansas City Chiefs. He retired in 1995. He was voted into the NFL's Hall of Fame in 2000. Many football experts consider Montana to be the best quarterback ever to play in the NFL.

Love of Sports

Sue worked three jobs to pay the family's bills. The family had little money to spend on sports equipment. Kurt and Matt played basketball with an old kickball and a homemade backboard. Kurt once tried to dunk the ball through the hoop. He tore the rim off the backboard.

Kurt attended Regis High School in Cedar Rapids. He played football, basketball, and baseball. Kurt did well in all three sports. In basketball, he led his district in rebounding in 11th and 12th grade. He also led his team to the state tournament in 12th grade. But the team lost in the first round.

Kurt started at quarterback for the football team in 11th grade. Gaylord Hauschildt was his coach. Hauschildt saw that Kurt had an excellent understanding of the game. He sometimes let Kurt call his own plays.

Kurt was invited to play in Iowa's Shrine Bowl after his 12th-grade season. The state's

Terry Allen of Northern Iowa was the only Division I-AA coach to recruit Kurt.

best high school football players take part in this game. Kurt was the quarterback for the North team. He led the team to victory and was named the game's MVP.

Going to Northern Iowa
Kurt wanted to play football at the University of Iowa. But the school's coaches were not

interested in him. No Division I colleges offered Kurt a scholarship.

The only coach who recruited Kurt was Northern Iowa's Terry Allen. Northern Iowa is a Division I-AA school located in Cedar Falls, Iowa. The school's teams are called the Panthers. Kurt was disappointed that no larger schools wanted him. But he also was excited to play for the Panthers. He thought he might get more playing time at a smaller school.

Kurt began his education at Northern Iowa in the fall of 1989. Allen told Kurt he would be a redshirt player during his first year. Kurt was allowed to practice with the team, but he could not play in games.

Kurt did not play in any games in 1990 or 1991. He did not like sitting on the bench. He worked hard to improve. He believed he would be the starting quarterback for the 1992 season. But Allen chose Jay Johnson as his starting quarterback instead. Kurt was disappointed. He thought about quitting

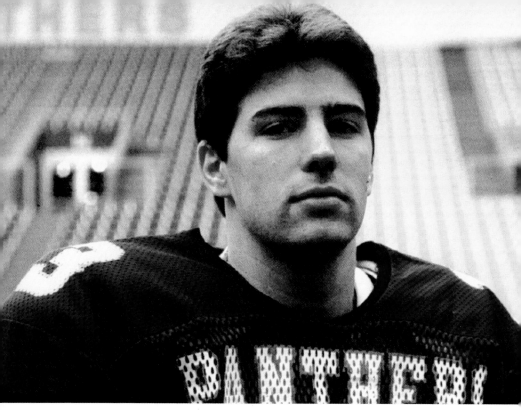

Kurt was named Gateway Conference Offensive Player of the Year for his final season at UNI.

football or going to a different school. But Kurt's parents talked him out of those ideas.

Final Season
The 1993 season was Kurt's last at Northern Iowa. He was finally named the team's starting quarterback. Kurt led the Panthers to an 8-3 record and to the playoffs.

The Panthers played Boston University in the first round. Boston University was undefeated and ranked fourth among all Division I-AA teams. The game was tied at 21 after regulation. In overtime, Kurt led the Panthers downfield for a field goal attempt. But kicker Scott Obermeier missed the 20-yard attempt. Boston University then scored a touchdown to win the game.

After the season, Kurt was named the Gateway Conference Offensive Player of the Year. He hoped his good season would give him a chance to play in the NFL.

Kurt met Brenda Meoni during his last year at Northern Iowa. Kurt and Brenda began to date. Kurt also spent time with Brenda's two children, Zachary and Jessie.

CHAPTER 3

Pro Ball

Four NFL teams invited Kurt to work out before the 1994 NFL draft. Kurt showed off his skills for teams in Green Bay, Cincinnati, Tampa Bay, and Atlanta. Kurt hoped his workouts would improve his chances of being drafted. Kurt watched the draft on TV. He stayed near his phone in case a team called him. But no teams called. None of the teams selected him.

NFL Failure
After the draft, four teams showed interest in Kurt. They were Green Bay, Tampa Bay,

Kurt hoped to join an NFL team after college.

> [Working at the grocery] was difficult and a humbling experience, but I think it really helped me to keep things in perspective.
> —Kurt Warner, CNNSI.com, 1/20/00

Cincinnati, and San Diego. Kurt agreed to join the Green Bay Packers. They paid him $5,000 to sign a contract.

In summer 1994, Kurt went to the Packers' training camp to learn the team's system. He tried to prove that he belonged in the NFL. But the Packers already had three quarterbacks on the roster. Kurt did not get many chances to play. The team cut him in August.

Kurt returned to Cedar Falls. He volunteered as an assistant coach for Northern Iowa. He moved in with Brenda, her parents, and her two children. He took care of the children during the day. He spent most of his evenings at Northern Iowa. At night, he worked at a grocery store. He stocked shelves, swept the floors, and bagged groceries.

The Barnstormers

In March 1995, the Iowa Barnstormers called Kurt. The Barnstormers were part of the Arena Football League (AFL). AFL teams play indoors on a 50-yard field. Kurt signed

Kurt believed he was good enough to play in the NFL.

a contract with the Barnstormers for $1,000
per game, plus bonuses. He then moved to
Des Moines to join the team.

Arena football was very different from the
game Kurt was used to playing. He played
poorly in his first two pre-season games. But
he quickly improved. He led the Barnstormers
to a 7-5 record. The team lost in the second
round of the playoffs.

In April 1996, Brenda's parents were killed in a tornado in Arkansas. The tragedy was difficult for Kurt and Brenda. Kurt had not been very religious until this time. But he and Brenda then decided to make religion a bigger part of their lives.

AFL Success

In 1996, Kurt began his second year with the Barnstormers. He led the team to a 12-2 record. The team then advanced to the Arena Bowl. They faced the Tampa Bay Storm.

The game was very close. The Barnstormers had the ball late in the second half. They trailed by four points. They moved down the field to the 1-yard line. But they could not score. The Storm won the game 42-38.

Kurt and the Barnstormers did not win the championship. But they were happy with their success. Kurt was named to the All-Arena-League team. The Barnstormers gave him a new contract worth more than $60,000 per year.

Kurt kept working to improve his skills.

> I have nothing but strong feelings for the Barnstormers. If things don't work out, I will sure want to come back if they will have me.
> —**Kurt Warner, *Des Moines Register*, 1/18/98**

In 1997, the Barnstormers were again one of the league's best teams. They went 11-3 in the regular season and advanced to the Arena Bowl. But the Arizona Rattlers beat the Barnstormers 55-33. It was Kurt's last game in the AFL.

Another Chance

In September, the Chicago Bears called Kurt. They wanted him to work out for the team's scouts. But Kurt and Brenda were preparing to get married that month. Kurt asked the Bears if they would wait until October for the workout.

After the wedding, Kurt and Brenda went on a trip to Jamaica. There, an insect or a scorpion stung Kurt's right elbow. He could not throw a football. Kurt called the Bears to reschedule his workout. But the Bears never called him back.

In 2000, the Barnstormers retired Kurt's jersey.

In December, Kurt worked out for the St. Louis Rams. The Rams signed him to a contract. They sent him to play for the Amsterdam Admirals in NFL Europe. Amsterdam is in the Netherlands. In early 1998, Kurt left his family in Des Moines and traveled to Europe.

Kurt played well for the Admirals. He led the league in yards, completions, and touchdowns. The Rams then asked Kurt to join them in training camp that summer. Kurt reported to training camp and began learning the Rams' systems. The Rams kept him on the team as the third-string quarterback. He was finally an NFL player.

Kurt signed a contract with the Rams in December 1997.

CHAPTER 4

The Big League

In 1998, Kurt was the Rams' scout-team quarterback. He led the scout offense. This unit of players practices against the team's defensive starters each week. Their job is to pretend to be the offense of the next opponent. Kurt pretended to be quarterbacks such as Dan Marino and Drew Bledsoe.

Kurt finally got his first snap in the NFL during the last game of the 1998 season. The Rams were trailing the San Francisco 49ers by 19 points in the final minutes. The Rams' coaches knew they could not win the game.

Kurt reported to the Rams' training camp in the summer of 1998.

They wanted to see Kurt perform in a game. Kurt completed four of 11 passes for 39 yards.

Starting Quarterback

In 1999, the Rams hired a new offensive coordinator named Mike Martz. Martz was hard on Kurt during training camp. He often yelled at Kurt and pointed out his mistakes in front of the team. But Martz also noticed Kurt's talent. He made Kurt the backup to starting quarterback Trent Green.

On August 28, Green suffered a knee injury in a pre-season game. Doctors told Green that he would not be able to play during the season. Rams' coach Dick Vermiel named Kurt as the new starting quarterback.

Kurt only had three days to prepare for his first NFL start. The Rams faced the Detroit Lions in another pre-season game. Kurt completed nine of 15 passes. He threw one touchdown pass.

Few football experts expected the Rams to be a good team during the regular season. The

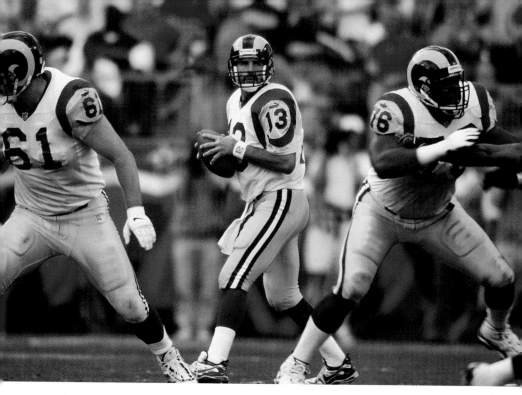

In 1999, the Rams named Kurt as the team's starting quarterback.

team had a 3-13 record in 1998. Kurt was an unknown quarterback. Most experts expected the Rams to finish the season in last place.

An Amazing Season

Kurt's first regular-season start came against the Baltimore Ravens. Many people questioned whether he was ready. Kurt quickly answered those questions. He threw for 309 yards and

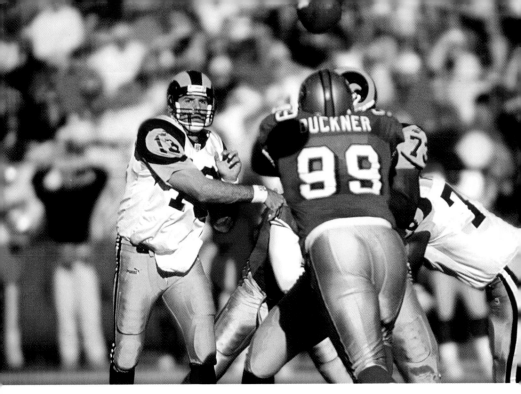

The Rams beat the San Francisco 49ers in their fourth game to improve their record to 4-0.

three touchdowns. The Rams won the game 27-10. After the game, Vermeil gave Kurt the game ball to reward him for his performance.

Kurt played well again in the Rams' second game against the Atlanta Falcons. He threw for 275 yards and three touchdowns. The Rams won the game 35-7. Kurt was later named the National Football Conference (NFC) Offensive Player of the Week.

Kurt threw for three touchdowns in the Rams' third game against the Cincinnati Bengals. He completed 17 of 21 passes for 310 yards in a 38-10 win.

The Rams were 3-0. Kurt was playing better than any quarterback in the NFL. But some experts still did not believe the Rams were a good team. The Rams had not played any of the NFL's best teams. The experts wanted to see how well the Rams would perform against a good team.

The Rams proved they were among the NFL's best teams in their fourth game. They played the San Francisco 49ers. The 49ers were one of the NFL's best teams. Kurt completed 20 of 23 passes for 323 yards and five touchdowns. The Rams won the game 42-20. Kurt had thrown 14 touchdown passes in his first four starts. No quarterback in NFL history had accomplished this feat.

Super Bowl Run

Kurt and the Rams continued their success throughout the regular season. They finished with a 13-3 record. They earned a first-round bye in the playoffs.

Kurt ended the season with 4,353 passing yards and 41 touchdown passes. He became the second NFL quarterback to throw more than 40 touchdown passes in a season. After the season, Kurt was named the NFL's MVP.

The Rams faced the Minnesota Vikings in the second round of the playoffs. The Vikings led the game at halftime. But the Rams came back in the second half and won the game 49-37. Kurt threw for 391 yards and five touchdowns.

The Rams faced the Tampa Bay Buccaneers in the NFC Championship. The Buccaneers led the game 6-5 with less than five minutes to play. Kurt then threw a 30-yard touchdown pass to receiver Ricky Proehl. The Rams won the game 11-5 and advanced to the Super Bowl.

The Rams completed their season with a 23-16 Super Bowl victory over the Titans. The next week, Kurt played for the NFC in the Pro Bowl.

Kurt and his teammates celebrated after they beat the Buccaneers to advance to the Super Bowl.

> The things that have affected me off the field have allowed me to realize that football is still just a game and there's going to be highs and lows just like there is in life.
> —Kurt Warner, CNNSI.com, 1/20/00

A Disappointing Season

Kurt and the Rams had another good start in the 2000 season. They won their first six games. Most football experts believed they were still the best team in the NFL. But Kurt hurt his throwing hand in a game against the Kansas City Chiefs. He missed several games because of the injury. The Rams won only four of their final 10 regular-season games. They lost to the New Orleans Saints in the first round of the playoffs.

Kurt was disappointed the Rams did not win more games. But he still had a great season. He completed more than 67 percent of his passes for 3,429 yards and 21 touchdowns.

In 2000, Kurt injured his hand during a game against the Chiefs.

CHAPTER 5

Kurt Warner Today

Kurt's MVP season made him one of the most popular players in the NFL. It also made him one of the highest-paid players. In 1999, Kurt's salary was $358,000. In 2000, he signed a seven-year contract for an average of more than $6.5 million per year.

Super Bowl Loss
The Rams were the most dominant team in the NFL for most of the 2001 season. They finished the regular season with a 14-2 record. Kurt threw for 4,830 yards and 36 touchdowns.

Kurt remains one of the best quarterbacks in the NFL today.

He was named the NFL's MVP for the second time in three years.

The Rams won their first two playoff games. They then faced the New England Patriots in the Super Bowl. Most NFL experts thought the Rams would easily win the game.

The Rams trailed the Patriots 17-10 late in the fourth quarter. Kurt then threw a 26-yard touchdown pass to wide receiver Ricky Proehl. The game was tied. The Patriots got the ball back and drove down the field. Kicker Adam Vinatieri then kicked a 48-yard field goal to give the Patriots a 20-17 victory. The Rams had lost in one of the biggest upsets in Super Bowl history.

Off the Field

Kurt enjoys spending time with his family during the off-season. Kurt adopted Brenda's two children in 1997. In 1999, Brenda and Kurt had a son named Cade.

Kurt and Brenda remember the life they led before Kurt's success with the Rams. They donate time and money to charities such as the

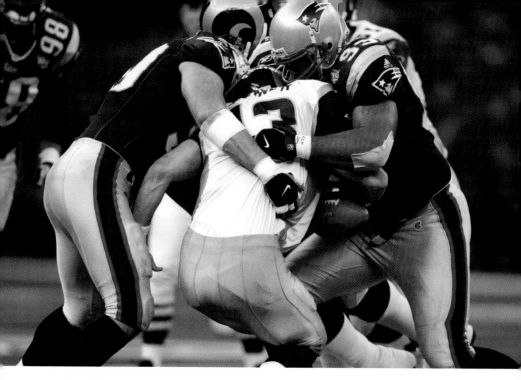

The Rams lost to the Patriots in one of the biggest upsets in Super Bowl history.

Red Cross to help people in need. Their son Zachary suffered brain damage in an accident as a baby. In 1999, Zachary spent time at a camp for children with special needs. Kurt was thankful for the way the camp helped Zachary. He has donated more than $200,000 to the camp.

Kurt says that he enjoys being a role model to children. He wants them to see that they can achieve their goals with hard work.

Career Highlights

1971—Kurt is born in Burlington, Iowa, on June 22.

1989—Kurt leads the North team to a victory in Iowa's Shrine Bowl; he is redshirted in his first year at Northern Iowa.

1993—Kurt becomes the starting quarterback at the University of Northern Iowa and is named the Gateway Conference Offensive Player of the Year.

1995—Kurt joins the Iowa Barnstormers of the Arena Football League.

1997—Kurt leads the Barnstormers to a second straight Arena Bowl and is named to the All-Arena-League Team.

1998—Kurt joins the Amsterdam Admirals of NFL Europe; he leads the league in almost every passing category; he joins the St. Louis Rams as the third-string quarterback.

1999—Kurt is named the Rams' starting quarterback; he leads the Rams to a 13-3 regular-season record.

2000—In January, the Rams defeat the Tennessee Titans in the Super Bowl; Kurt is named Super Bowl MVP.

2001—Kurt throws for 4,830 yards and 36 touchdowns and is named the NFL's MVP.

2002—In February, the New England Patriots defeat the Rams in the Super Bowl.

Words to Know

autobiography (aw-toh-bye-OG-ruh-fee)—a book in which the author tells the story of his or her life

contract (KON-trakt)—an agreement between an owner and a player; contracts determine players' salaries.

endorse (en-DORSS)—to sponsor a product by appearing in advertisements

recruit (ri-KROOT)—to try to convince someone to join a team; college football coaches recruit high school players to play on their teams.

redshirt (RED-shurt)—a term to describe a college athlete who may practice with a team but may not participate in competition

To Learn More

Bailer, Darice. *Touchdown!: Great Quarterbacks in Football History.* Step into Reading. New York: Random House, 1999.

Dougherty, Terri. *Kurt Warner.* Jam Session. Edina, Minn.: Abdo & Daughters, 2000.

Stewart, Mark. *Kurt Warner: Can't Keep Him Down.* Football's New Wave. Brookfield, Conn.: Millbrook Press, 2001.

Useful Addresses

Kurt Warner
c/o The St. Louis Rams
1 Rams Way
Earth City, MO 63045

Pro Football Hall of Fame
2121 George Halas Drive NW
Canton, OH 44708

Internet Sites

ESPN.com—Kurt Warner
http://football.espn.go.com/nfl/players/
   profile?statsId=4541

Iowa's Kurt Warner
http://DesMoinesRegister.com/sports/extras/warner

NFL.com
http://nfl.com

St. Louis Rams
http://www.stlouisrams.com

Index